HAL LEONARD BASS UKULELE METHOD

BY LYNN AND FRED SOKOLOW

Editorial Assistance by Ronny S. Schiff
Photos by Debra Avery
Front cover image courtesy of Flight Instruments

The Recording
Bass Ukulele: Lynn Sokolow
Additional Instruments and Vocals: Fred Sokolow
Sound Engineer: Michael Monagan
Recorded and Mixed at Sossity Sound

The audio tracks are mixed so that the bass ukulele is on one side of your
stereo and the other instruments and voice are on the other side. Use the
PLAYBACK+ audio player to pan out the featured bass uke part and play along!

PLAYBACK+
Speed • Pitch • Balance • Loop

To access audio visit:
www.halleonard.com/mylibrary

Enter Code
1442-6674-2865-1440

T0057805

ISBN 978-1-70510-577-1

Visit Hal Leonard Online at
www.halleonard.com

World headquarters, contact:
Hal Leonard
7777 West Bluemound Road
Milwaukee, WI 53213
Email: info@halleonard.com

In Europe, contact:
Hal Leonard Europe Limited
42 Wigmore Street
Marylebone, London, W1U 2RY
Email: info@halleonardeurope.com

In Australia, contact:
Hal Leonard Australia Pty. Ltd.
4 Lentara Court
Cheltenham, Victoria, 3192 Australia
Email: info@halleonard.com.au

CONTENTS

SONG LIST
(in order of appearance)

INTRODUCTION

In recent years, with the incredible worldwide popularity of the ukulele, more and more ukulele players are becoming interested in the bass uke.

Here's the thing about bass: after learning the basics of the instrument, not only will you be able to jump into any group of players, in any style of music, but you will emerge a hero! Players need you, whether they know it or not. It doesn't matter how accomplished they are, or how many of them might be in a group… they still need you.

This phenomenon is easy to demonstrate. Try joining a uke group (or any "bass-less" group of players). Let them start strumming and singing without you, and then join in. All of a sudden, the music has a depth, a fullness that was absent without you. Like the foundation on a house, you are what everyone else builds on. You keep the time, you set the feel, and you provide the groove. Even when you play very simple bass lines, you make any ensemble sound better. Trust us, you'll be the hero!

In this book, you start from the absolute beginning. Nothing will be over your head. You will learn to accompany all kinds of music, in any key, from the simplest bass lines to funky grooves—it's all here. So, jump in and you'll be surprised how quickly you can play with other people and how much fun you'll have.

Good luck!

Lynn and Fred Sokolow

PRELIMINARIES

PARTS OF THE BASS UKULELE

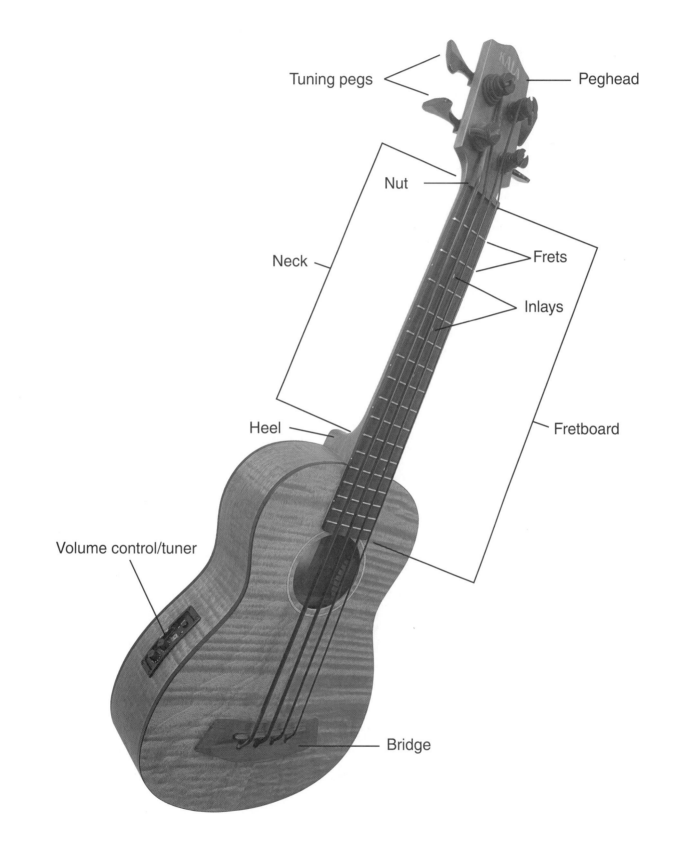

Tuning pegs

Peghead

Nut

Neck

Frets

Inlays

Heel

Fretboard

Volume control/tuner

Bridge

Note: Some bass ukes are fretless, like the double bass, but if you're a beginner to the instrument, get one with frets!

HOW TO HOLD IT

When sitting, you can rest the bass uke across your leg or on your lap, as shown below; find a position that is comfortable for you.

STRAP IT ON

Many people find a strap helpful, especially when standing. If you use a strap while sitting, your right arm is free because you don't have to hold up the uke.

STRINGS: STEEL OR POLYURETHANE

Most bass ukuleles come with polyurethane strings, but metal-wound strings are also available. Here's how the two types compare:

- Polyurethane strings are a bit easier on the fretting hand. A minor downside is that they take longer to "break in" (stretch)—about two weeks.

- Metal-wound strings have a brighter sound and resemble electric bass strings. They are much more expensive than polyurethane strings.

TUNERS

Many bass ukes have built-in tuners. If yours does not, many electronic tuners are available that clip onto the uke headstock. You can find tuner apps on smartphones, but you have to balance the phone on your lap or put it on a desk or music stand. Free online tuners are also available.

Built-In

Clip-On

CASES

Whether it's a hardshell case or canvas gig bag, a case makes your bass uke easier to carry and protects it when you travel. A case can also carry accessories, like strings and cables.

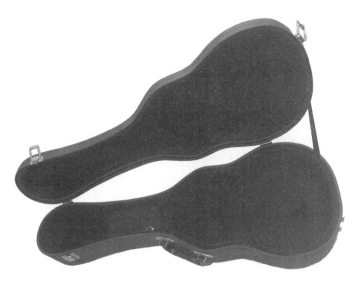

Hardshell

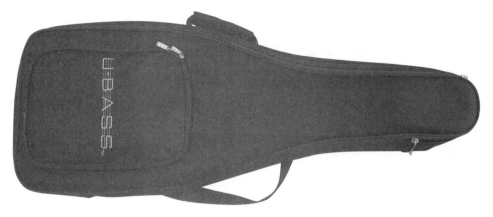

Gig Bag

Carrying a Gig Bag

ELECTRIC CABLES

The bass uke makes hardly any sound unless plugged into an amplifier; that's why it has a built-in pickup. You need a guitar cable, which you should carry in your case along with some extra strings! Cables come in different lengths: six-, eight-, or ten-feet long if you plan to sit or stand near your amplifier, and longer if you plan to play on a stage.

AMPLIFIERS

There are all kinds of small and large amplifiers. Some are made specifically for bass ukes, and some are much more powerful than others. Again, your choice depends on how you plan to use your bass uke.

MUSICAL SYMBOLS

Don't panic! You don't have to learn to read music notation to use this book... if you already know how to read tablature, you can skip to page 11. If you do want to learn to read music notation, carry on!

Music is written with notes on a **staff**. The staff has five lines and four spaces between the lines. Where a note is written on the staff determines its pitch (highness or lowness). At the beginning of the staff is a **clef sign**. Bass ukulele music is written in the **bass clef**.

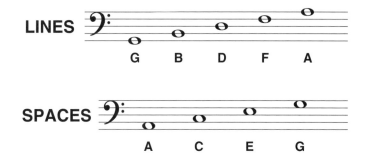

Each line and space of the staff has a letter name. The **lines** are (from bottom to top) G–B–D–F–A, which you can remember as "**G**ood **B**oys **D**o **F**ine **A**lways." The **spaces** are (from bottom to top) A–C–E–G, which can be remembered as "**A**ll **C**ows **E**at **G**rass."

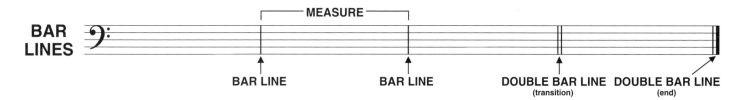

The staff is divided into several parts by **bar lines**. The space between two bar lines is called a **measure** (also known as a "bar"). At the end of a piece of music, a **double bar line** is placed on the staff.

Each measure contains a group of **beats**. Beats are the steady pulse of music. You respond to the pulse or beat when you tap your foot.

The two numbers placed next to the clef sign are the **time signature**. The top number tells you how many beats are in a single measure.

FOUR BEATS PER MEASURE
QUARTER NOTE (♩) GETS ONE BEAT

The bottom number of the time signature tells you what kind of note will receive one beat.

Note values indicate the length (number of counts) of a musical sound.

| NOTE VALUES | WHOLE NOTE = 4 BEATS | HALF NOTE = 2 BEATS | QUARTER NOTE = 1 BEAT | EIGHTH NOTE = ½ BEAT | SIXTEENTH NOTE = ¼ BEAT |

When different kinds of notes are placed on different lines or spaces, you will know the pitch of the note and how long to play the sound.

TIES, RESTS, AND TIME SIGNATURES

Before you start to get into some really great music, take a moment to familiarize yourself with a few standard music symbols that you'll encounter as you work your way through this book.

Rests

Music is made up of both sound and silence. Silence is represented by musical symbols called **rests**. They are just as important as the notes you play. Each type of note has a corresponding rest of the same name and duration:

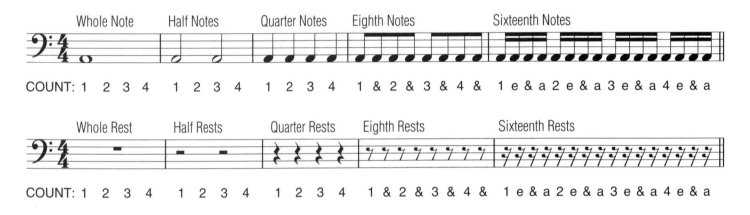

In the staff above the rests, notice that consecutive eighth notes and sixteenth notes are **beamed** together in groups. Eighth notes have single beams, while sixteenth notes have double beams.

Dotted Notes

When you see a **dotted note**, hold that note 50% longer than you normally would. For example, a dotted half note ($\dot{\math{d}}$) lasts as long as a half note plus a quarter note. A dot adds half the value of the note.

3 beats = 2 beats + 1 beat

Ties

Another standard music symbol that you will often encounter is the **tie** (⌣). When you see two (or more) notes tied together, play them as a single note. In other words, simply add the first note to the second and hold them out for the full duration of both notes. Only the first note of a group of tied notes is plucked. Sometimes, ties can even extend across multiple measures.

1 beat + 1 beat = 2 beats

GETTING STARTED

TUNING

The four bass ukulele strings are numbered. The string that is highest in pitch—the thinnest string—is the 1st string. The string that is lowest in pitch—the thickest string—is the 4th string. They are tuned like this:

4th string: E
3rd string: A
2nd string: D
1st string: G

Using an electronic tuner, pluck a string and listen to its pitch while turning its tuning peg. Usually, the tuner will indicate with a green light or something similar when the pitch is correct. Of course, you can also tune by ear to the pitches given on the audio track.

TRACK 1

To access audio, head over to www.halleonard.com/mylibrary
and input the code found on page 1!

THE PLUCKING HAND

Most bass players pluck the strings with their right-hand fingers (index and middle), rather than using a pick. They brace their plucking hand with their thumb:

TABLATURE

In **tablature** (or "tab") notation, the horizontal lines represent strings, and the numbers indicate which fret to play (0 = open).

Bracing your plucking hand as shown in the previous photo, pluck each open string four times while following the notation below. The standard notation staff is on top, and the tablature staff is on the bottom. Notice the **ledger line** on the E notes. When notes go above or below the staff, we use ledger lines to help see their location more easily.

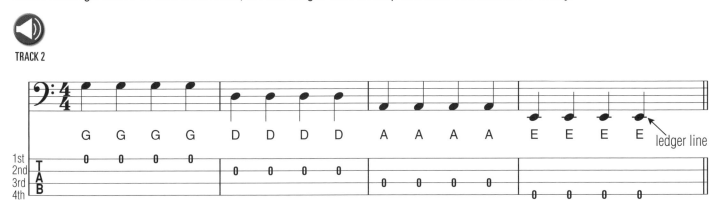

TRACK 2

THE FRETTING HAND

When fretting a string, press down with your left hand (if you're right-handed) near the fret wire—just to the left of it—without touching it. Press hard enough to get a clear tone. It helps to have short fingernails!

The fingers of the fretting hand are numbered like this:

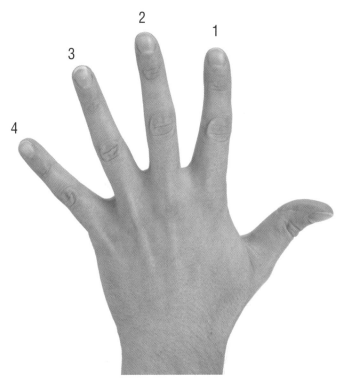

Sustain and Staccato

Sometimes you want a plucked string to ring out, or **sustain**. Other times you want to cut it short by muting the string—this is called **staccato**.

- To keep an *open* string from ringing out, mute it by lightly resting any finger of your fretting hand on the string.

- To keep a *fretted* string from ringing out, lift your fretting finger up, lightly, while it's still on the string.

BOTH HANDS AT ONCE!

Practice playing an open A string. Pluck it four times, letting each note ring out (sustain) for its full value.

TRACK 3

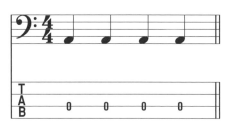

Practice playing the same open A string, but play it staccato by quickly muting the string with your fretting hand right after plucking each note. In written music, staccato is indicated by a dot above or below the note.

TRACK 3 (cont.)

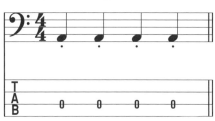

Practice playing the A string at the 5th fret, which is the note D. Fret the string with your index finger. Let the first four notes ring out for their full value, and then play the next four notes staccato.

TRACK 3 (cont.)

Hurray, you're already playing bass ukulele with both hands! To take things a step further, pluck each open string four times, alternating between regular (sustained) notes and staccato notes.

TRACK 4

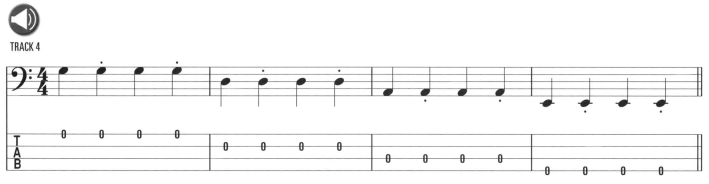

Now, do the same thing, but fret each string at the 5th fret.

TRACK 4 (cont.)

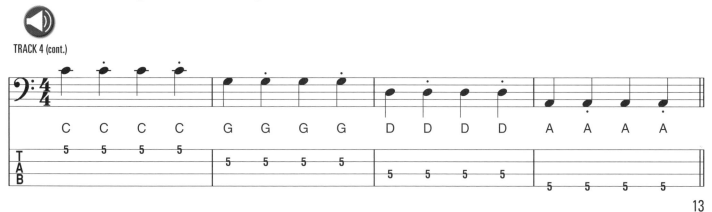

PLAYING A BASS LINE

Now, you're ready to play a simple bass line! Here's a familiar one to get you started. The first two times you play the line, let the notes ring out. Play the notes staccato the next two times.

STRAY CAT STRUT

Words and Music by Brian Setzer

TRACK 5

Did you notice the new musical symbol in the song's notation? There's a B♭ note (pronounced "B flat"), which is a note that's one fret lower than the B note. You'll learn more about flats and sharps in the next section.

Besides the Stray Cats' hit tune, this bass line is also used in "Hit the Road, Jack" (Ray Charles), "Like a Hurricane" (Neil Young), "Sultans of Swing" (Dire Straits), and other popular songs.

IT'S UP TO UKE

Sustain and staccato are often a part of your own personal interpretation of a piece of music. You won't always see indications for these in the music. Experiment with both to see what works best for any given bass line.

DIFFERENT RHYTHMS

The chart below shows several different rhythms, using animal names and counting numbers to express the note values. This is a quick way to get you playing some cool bass lines right off the "bat."

Rhythm Chart

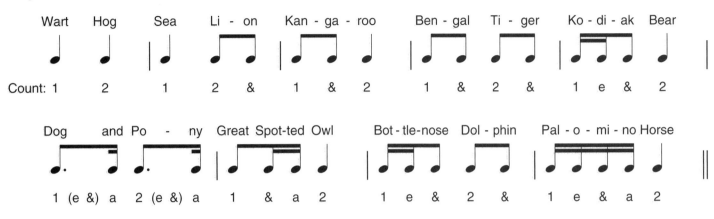

Play the "Stray Cat Strut" bass line using some of these rhythms. Notice the new bar lines with dots in the notation. These are **repeat signs**, which tell you to repeat all the written music between them. In this example, the repeats tell you to play each two-measure phrase twice (without pausing) before moving on to the next phrase. Listen to the audio track and follow along with the notation to understand how they work.

TRACK 6

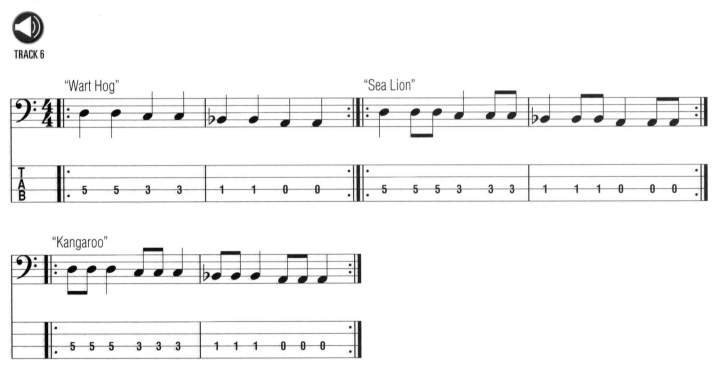

Now that you've got the mechanics down and both hands working, it's time to build some bass lines.

BUILDING BASS LINES

Bass lines are always determined by the chords in a song. You can never go wrong if you play the **root** note of each chord. The root is the note a chord is built on, and it gives the chord its name (like a C note in a C chord). That's why you need to learn the notes on the fretboard before you start playing bass lines.

Don't panic! You don't have to learn all the notes at once. You already know at least four notes—the four open strings.

E (4th string, open)

A (3rd string, open)

D (2nd string, open)

G (1st string, open)

Now, to introduce you to the other notes, we'll start with the 4th and 3rd strings, and only go up five frets.

NOTES ON THE 4TH STRING

SHARPS AND FLATS

The symbol # is a **sharp**, and it means "one fret higher." ("Higher" means "away from the nut, toward the bridge" because the notes get higher in pitch when you go in that direction on a string.) The F# note is one fret above the F note, and the G# is one fret above the G note. The distance of one fret on a string is a **half step**.

The symbol ♭ is a **flat**, and it means "one fret lower." G♭ is one fret below G, and A♭ is one fret below A. So, the notes that are between the **natural** (unaltered) notes (A, B, C, D, E, F, G) each have two names. F# is the same note as G♭. G# is the same note as A♭. The notes would be written differently in standard notation, but in tab, they're exactly the same.

Notice that most of the natural notes (F, G, A) are two frets (**whole step**) apart, but E and F are only one fret apart. For our purposes in this book, there is no E# or F♭.

Now, look at the 4th-string notes on a fretboard diagram. Memorize these notes. Some people find it helpful in the beginning to put small stickers with note names on the neck of their bass uke.

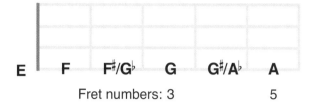

NOTES ON THE 3RD STRING

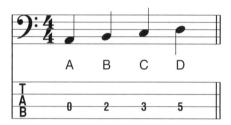

As you can see, some notes can be played in different places on the bass uke—for example, the A note on the 5th fret of the 4th string and the A note on the open 3rd string. In these cases, the tab tells you exactly where to play the note.

Now, look at the 3rd-string notes on a fretboard diagram, including the sharp and flat notes as well.

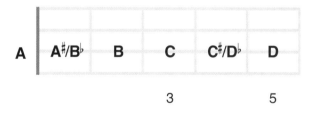

As you can see from the fretboard chart, there is no # or ♭ between B and C—those notes are one fret apart. Memorize the notes shown on this chart!

We'll look at the notes on the 2nd and 1st strings soon, but first, use what you've just learned to play a song.

FINALLY—PLAYING A WHOLE SONG!

As already mentioned, you can back up any song on bass uke just by playing the root notes. For example, here is Vance Joy's hit "Riptide" in the key of C. The song has three chords: C, G, and A minor (Am). Using quarter notes (one beat for each note), play the root of each chord and count "1, 2, 3, 4." There are four beats in each measure. In the first measure, you'll play A on beats 1 and 2 and G on beats 3 and 4. In the second measure, you'll play C for four quarter notes. You'll do the same for measures 3 and 4.

RIPTIDE (Key of C)

Words and Music by Vance Joy

TRACK 7

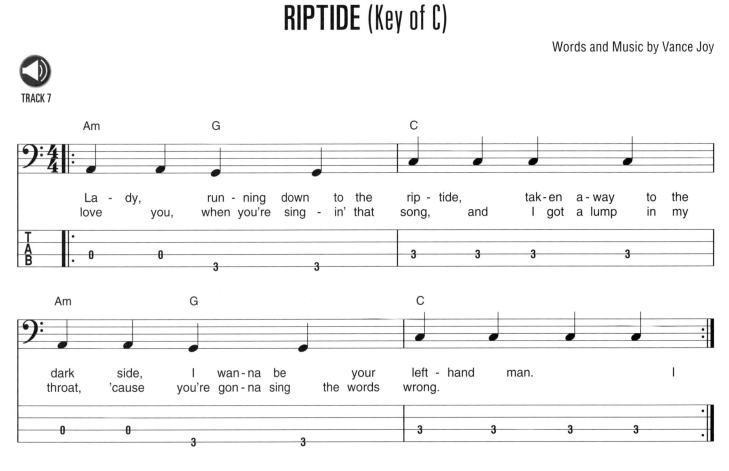

NOTES ON THE 2ND STRING

Now, look at the 2nd-string notes on a fretboard diagram, including the sharp and flat notes as well.

NOTES ON THE 1ST STRING

Now, look at the 1st-string notes on a fretboard diagram, including the sharp and flat notes.

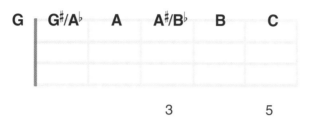

KEYS AND KEY SIGNATURES

- Songs are in various **keys**. The key of a song is its basic tonality, and it is taken from a scale that has the same name. For instance, the key of C major—or simply, the key of C—is made up of the notes and chords taken from the C major scale. (We'll discuss the major scale shortly.)

- A **key signature** appears at the beginning of every line of music. It indicates the key by telling you which notes are sharp or flat throughout the song. For example, the key of C has no sharps or flats, and the key of G has one sharp, F#.

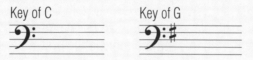

Now that you know the notes on all the strings and you've learned about keys and key signatures, let's play "Riptide" in the key of G.

RIPTIDE (Key of G)

Words and Music by Vance Joy

TRACK 7 (cont.)

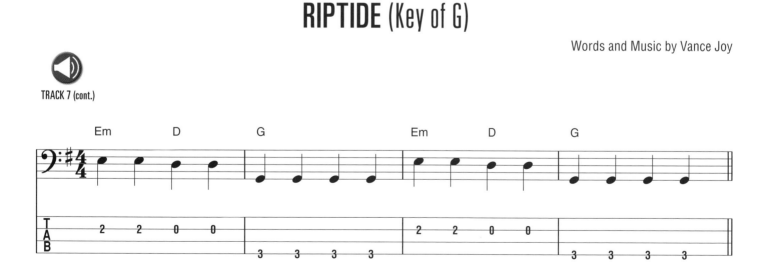

USING SCALES

THE MAJOR SCALE

A **scale** is a series of notes in a particular order of whole steps and half steps. There are many different kinds of scales, but in terms of understanding basic music theory, the **major scale** is the most important type.

The notes of the major scale are arranged in the order of whole step, whole step, half step, whole step, whole step, whole step, and half step. There are seven notes in a major scale, with the eighth note being the **octave** of the first note (same note but higher in pitch). In a major scale, the first note is the **tonic**. The notes of the scale can also be referred to by their **scale degrees**: 1–2–3–4–5–6–7–8.

For example, here is the C major scale:

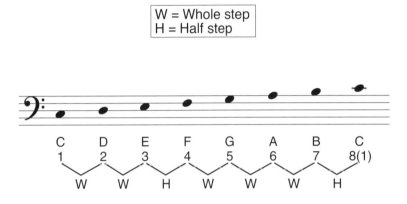

Note: Chords come from scales. Because of this, chord roots and scale tonics can sometimes be thought of in the same way. The root is the first or bottom note in a chord, and the tonic is the first or lowest note in a scale.

ALTERNATING BASS (ROOT–5TH)

The first step beyond playing only the chord roots is alternating between the root and the **5th**. The 5th is the fifth note in the major scale. For example, C is the root of a C chord, and the fifth note in the C major scale is G; so, G is the 5th.

Here's the good news: you don't have to learn what the 5th of every scale is and memorize it. You don't even have to know what note you're playing to find the 5th. The chart below shows an easy way to find the 5th of any note: whichever string you're playing, the note at the same fret on the string right below it is the 5th ("below," as in "the 4th string is below the 3rd string").

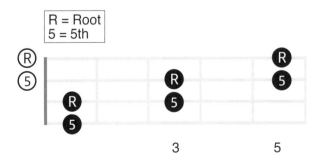

Now, return to the "Stray Cat Strut" progression to make it a little fancier, alternating between the root and 5th of each chord.

STRAY CAT STRUT (Alternating Bass 1)

Words and Music by Brian Setzer

You may be wondering, "How do I find the 5th if my root is on the 4th string?" There are two ways to find the 5th. In the way we just covered, the 5th is on the string *below* the root. You can also find the 5th on the string *above* the root, two frets higher. The diagram below shows this method of finding a 5th when the root is on the 4th, 3rd, or 2nd string.

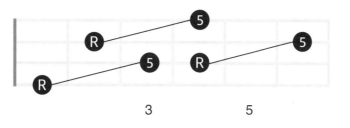

With this root–5th pattern, fret the root with your 1st finger and the 5th with your 3rd finger.

This method works for open-string roots as well:

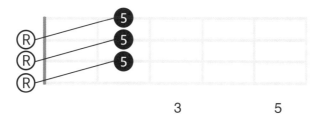

Here's the "Stray Cat Strut" bass line using the approach shown in the previous two diagrams. **Note:** In the first measure, there's a new way to play the A note; it's on the 7th fret of the 2nd string.

STRAY CAT STRUT (Alternating Bass 2)

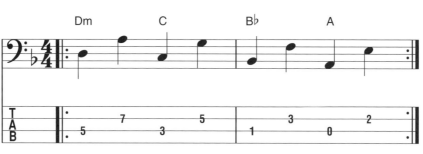

Cut time is indicated with the time signature ¢, and it is equivalent to 2/2. In cut time, the note and rest values are cut in half, so there are two beats per measure and the half note receives the beat.

Now that you know how to play alternating bass using roots and 5ths, congratulations—you're a bass player! You can play thousands of songs in just about any genre and not hit one bad note. All you need to know is what the chords are. For instance, start with a simple two-chord song, Hank Williams' "Jambalaya (On the Bayou)," which has been recorded by close to a hundred artists. Here's a bass accompaniment for it in the key of D, using open strings. As promised, the bass uke just alternates between the root and 5th throughout. The first half of the verse alternates between the root and the 5th on the string below it, and the second half alternates between the root and the 5th on the string above it.

TRACK 10

JAMBALAYA (ON THE BAYOU) (Key of D)

Words and Music by Hank Williams

Here's the same tune in the key of C. We're still alternating between the roots and 5ths using the two previous approaches, but now we're playing fretted strings.

JAMBALAYA (ON THE BAYOU) (Key of C)

Words and Music by Hank Williams

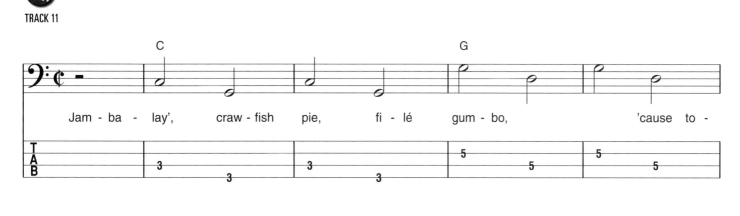

TRACK 11

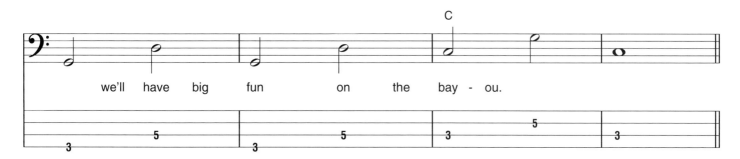

Since the "Jambalaya" accompaniment is played on fretted strings, you could move it up or down the fretboard to play the exact same arrangement in any key. Try it in D, for example, by moving that arrangement up two frets.

Jason Mraz's pop hit "I'm Yours" is a four-chord song. Here it is in the key of C, using both alternating-bass approaches.

I'M YOURS

Words and Music by Jason Mraz

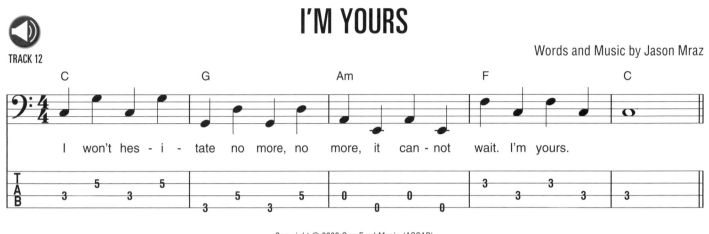

TRACK 12

PLAYING ROOT–5TH–OCTAVE–5TH

Here's a step beyond playing just the root and 5th: root–5th–octave–5th. Remember, an octave note is the eighth note of a major scale. It's the same note as the root note, only an octave higher. Since a C major scale is C–D–E–F–G–A–B–C, the last C is an octave above the first C.

If that confuses you, don't worry! What you really need to know about octaves is illustrated in the diagram below. It shows you how to find an octave note quickly and easily, without having to count or think about it.

Octaves

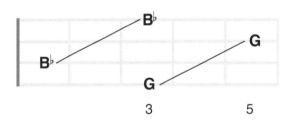

As the diagram shows, your octave note is always two strings higher and two frets higher. This is true for the 4th and 2nd strings, as well as for the 3rd and 1st strings. Here's the fret-hand fingering for the root–5th–octave–5th pattern in two locations. The octave note is indicated with the number 8.

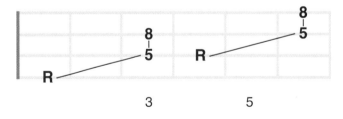

Bonus: By knowing the notes on the 3rd and 4th strings, you can easily figure out the notes on the 1st and 2nd strings—just by using this method of finding octaves.

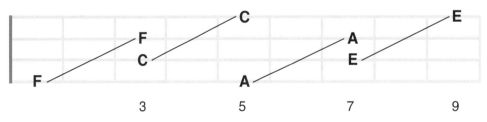

1ST AND 2ND ENDINGS

1st and 2nd endings are indicated in music notation with the numbers "1" and "2" under brackets. When you see these, like in the next song example, play the 1st ending and then repeat from the beginning; when you get to the 1st ending again, skip over it and play the 2nd ending.

Now, play "Jambalaya" and "I'm Yours" using the root–5th–octave–5th pattern.

JAMBALAYA (ON THE BAYOU)
(Root–5th–Octave–5th)

Words and Music by Hank Williams

TRACK 13

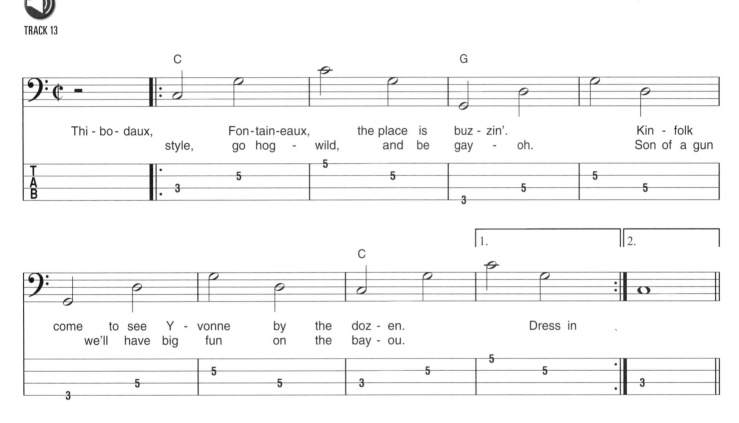

I'M YOURS (Root–5th–Octave–5th)

Words and Music by Jason Mraz

TRACK 14

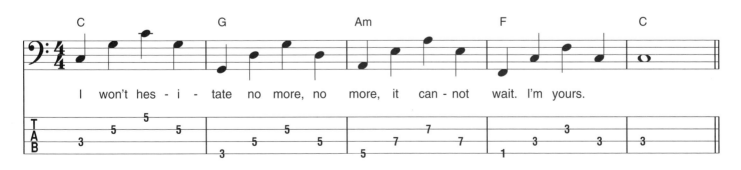

CONNECTING RUNS

Let's face it—playing just roots, 5ths, and octaves can get a little monotonous. One way to make it a bit more interesting is to add simple connecting runs. They sound good when you change chords, and sometimes you can play them when a song stays on a chord for a few bars.

Play the following licks that go back and forth from C to G and C to F. Practice them in a loop to get really comfortable with them. The second half of the example shows the same connecting runs with no open strings. Because there are no open strings, they're movable; they can be played all over the fretboard. You can also move them up a string, as shown in the last part of the example.

TRACK 15

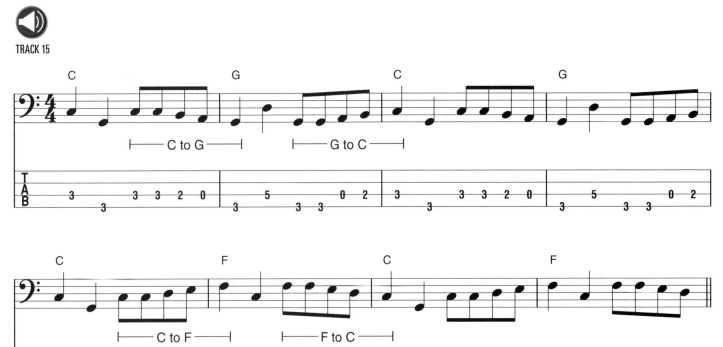

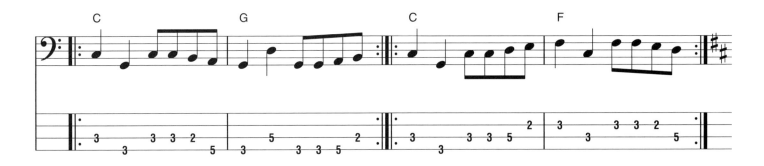

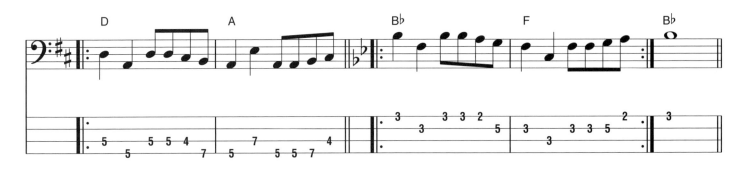

These connecting runs go up and down the major scale of the key you're playing in. For example, if you're in the key of C and going from a C to an F chord, you play scale tones 1–2–3–4 (C–D–E–F).

Now, look at some variations on these runs using the tune "Jambalaya" in the key of C. Notice in the second half of the song, you can play the root of the chord as a half note—instead of two quarter notes—before the connecting run. Also, notice in measure 8 that you can use one of these runs to add interest to your bass line when you are staying on one chord for several measures.

JAMBALAYA (ON THE BAYOU)
(Bass Runs)

Words and Music by Hank Williams

TRACK 16

The **shuffle feel** is used often in blues, jazz, and folk music. As opposed to a straight-eighth (rock) feel, it uses **swing eighth notes**. These have a *triplet* feel in which each beat is divided into three equal parts, rather than two. Swing eighths have a long-short, long-short, "bump-ba-bump-ba-bump" feel. They look like regular eighth notes, but the shuffle rhythm is indicated at the beginning of the music with the words "Shuffle Feel" or "Swing Feel."

The next example has a shuffle feel. Make sure to listen to the audio to get familiar with this important rhythm.

VARYING THE RHYTHM

Remember when you played variations of the "Stray Cat Strut" bass part using the "animal" Rhythm Chart? You can also take what you just learned (root–5th and root–5th–octave–5th) and vary the rhythms slightly. Try this by revisiting "Jambalaya" and "I'm Yours."

In every other measure of "Jambalaya," we'll use a dotted quarter note followed by an eighth note to vary the rhythm. Play the dotted quarter note on beat 1 and the eighth note on the "&" of beat 2.

JAMBALAYA (ON THE BAYOU)
(Root—5th with Rhythm Variations)

Words and Music by Hank Williams

TRACK 17

This version of "I'm Yours" uses the Wart-Hog and Kodiak Bear rhythms (from the Rhythm Chart). Notice here that the shuffle feel is given to the sixteenth notes. Be sure to check out the audio for this one.

I'M YOURS
(Root—5th—Octave—5th with Rhythm Variations)

Words and Music by Jason Mraz

TRACK 18

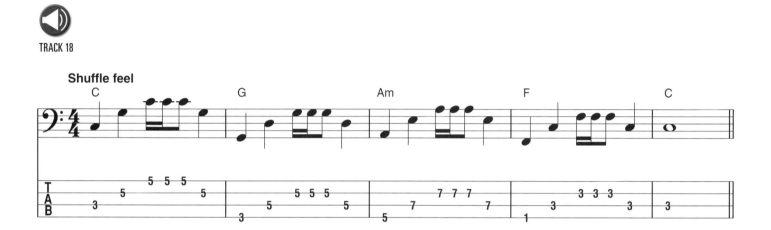

THE NEXT STEP IN BUILDING BASS LINES

Where do you go from here? As you saw in the last chapter, you can't go wrong by playing the root of each chord, the root and 5th, or the root, 5th, and octave. But if that's all you do, your bass lines may be a tad repetitive. So, it's time to add more elements.

PLAYING ROOT–3RD–5TH–3RD (MAJOR ARPEGGIOS)

When you play the notes of a chord in succession, it's called an **arpeggio**. You already played bass lines by alternating the root and the 5th. Now, you're going to add the **3rd** from the major scale and play root–3rd–5th–3rd. These three notes make a major chord, so root–3rd–5th–3rd is a **major arpeggio**.

There are two kinds of 3rds you need to know about here: **major 3rd** and **minor 3rd**. The major arpeggio has the major 3rd. You can always find the major 3rd by going up two whole steps (four frets) on any string, including open strings:

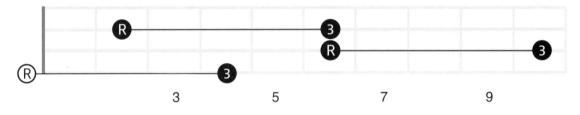

Here's what the major arpeggio looks like on the fretboard:

Here are some major arpeggios to play on the famous blues tune "Kansas City," in the key of A. You'll be using open strings for the roots of the song's three chords (A, D, and E).

KANSAS CITY

Words and Music by Jerry Leiber and Mike Stoller

TRACK 19

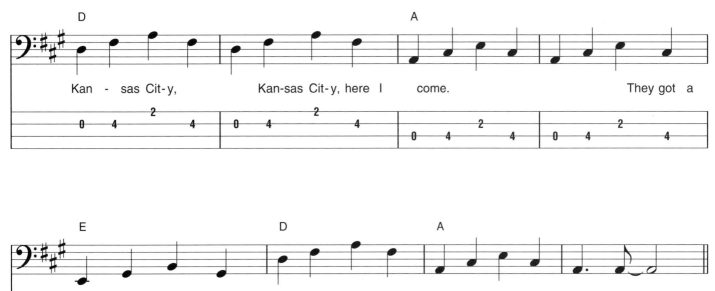

Kan - sas Cit-y,   Kan-sas Cit-y, here I   come.   They got a

cra-zy way of lov-in' there and I'm gon-na get me some.

WALKING BASS

Congratulations! You've graduated from playing alternating root–5th type bass lines; now, you're playing **walking bass**, a series of notes outlining the chord changes in a steady rhythm. It's heard in blues, swing, jazz, and even country and bluegrass music.

You can also find the major 3rd by going up a string and down a fret. Here's another way to play major arpeggios:

The following version of "Kansas City" uses the major arpeggio shapes you just learned. There are no open strings here, so you can move this arrangement up or down the neck and play in many different keys.

KANSAS CITY
(Movable)

Words and Music by Jerry Leiber and Mike Stoller

TRACK 20

Here's a major arpeggio walking bass line for "Blueberry Hill," in the key of G. Notice the rhythmic variation. It's the same arpeggio as in "Kansas City" but with a different rhythmic feel.

BLUEBERRY HILL

Words and Music by Al Lewis,
Larry Stock and Vincent Rose

MINOR ARPEGGIOS

You've just learned how to play a major arpeggio by playing root–3rd–5th–3rd. Minor chords have a flatted 3rd (♭3), otherwise known as a **minor 3rd**. A minor 3rd is one fret lower than a major 3rd. So, a **minor arpeggio** is played: root–♭3rd–5th–♭3rd. You can always find the minor 3rd by going up a string and down two frets. Play the root with your 2nd finger and the minor 3rd with your 1st finger (or no finger if on an open string).

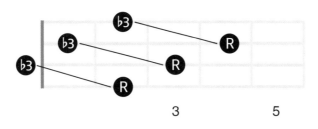

You can also find the minor 3rd by going up three frets on a string. Play the root with your 1st finger and the minor 3rd with your 4th finger (or in the case of an open-string root, play the root with no finger and the minor 3rd with your 3rd finger).

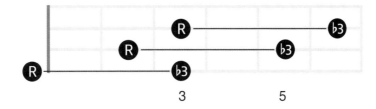

Here are three ways to play a minor arpeggio.

TRACK 22

Here's a song to help you practice your minor arpeggios. R.E.M.'s pop hit "Losing My Religion" is in a minor key and includes some major chords as well. As you would expect, you play minor arpeggios on the minor chords and major arpeggios on the major chords. This bass uke accompaniment to the first verse of "Losing My Religion" shows two ways to play minor arpeggios; the first part of the example includes open-string root notes (measures 1–9), and the remainder has fretted root notes (measures 10–17). There are also some rhythmic variations that make the bass line more interesting.

LOSING MY RELIGION

Words and Music by William Berry, Peter Buck,
Michael Mills and Michael Stipe

TRACK 23

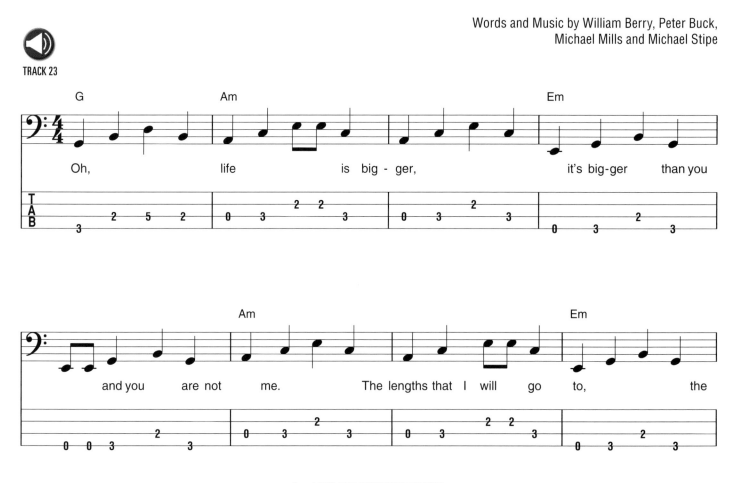

ADDING THE 6TH

By adding the **6th** note of the major scale to a major arpeggio, you get a really cool walking bass line that you've heard in countless songs. Your arpeggio is now twice as long: root–3rd–5th–6th–8th–6th–5th–3rd. You can play it all over the fretboard if you start on the 4th or 3rd string at the 2nd fret or higher.

The 6th of the major scale is one string above the major 3rd at the same fret:

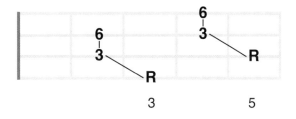

Notice that the pattern above works whether you start with the root on the 4th string or the 3rd string.

Adding the 6th to your arpeggio extends the walking bass line, like this:

Key of G

Key of C

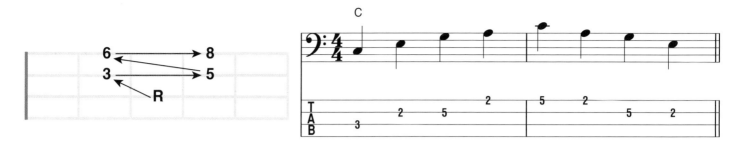

This walking bass line works well for swing and blues tunes. Try it on "Kansas City."

KANSAS CITY
(Walking Bass with 6ths)

TRACK 24

Words and Music by Jerry Leiber and Mike Stoller

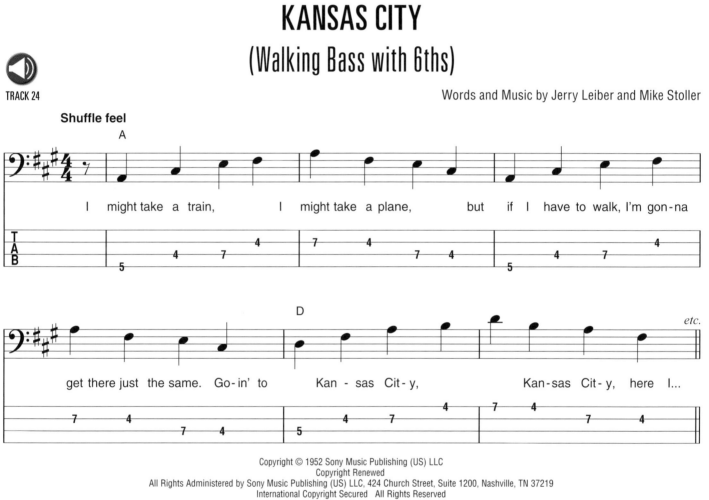

I might take a train, I might take a plane, but if I have to walk, I'm gon-na

get there just the same. Go-in' to Kan - sas Cit-y, Kan-sas Cit-y, here I...

The pattern is different if you start on an open string:

Key of E   ## Key of A

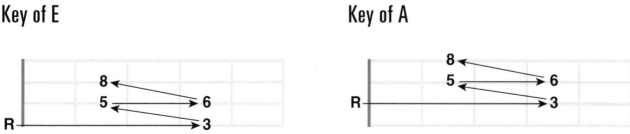

Now, try this pattern on "Kansas City."

KANSAS CITY
(Open-String Root/Walking Bass with 6ths)

Words and Music by Jerry Leiber and Mike Stoller

TRACK 25

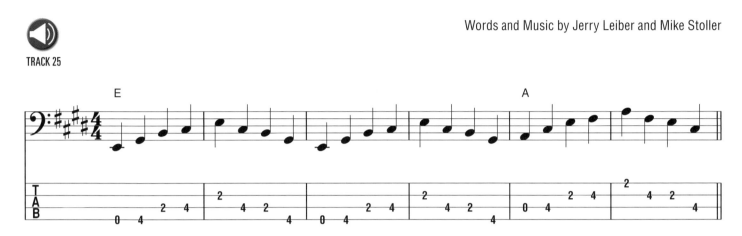

If you're getting tired of all the variations of "Kansas City," you can use the same bass lines on hundreds of other familiar songs like "Hound Dog," "Johnny B. Goode," "Whole Lotta Shakin' Goin' On," "Blue Suede Shoes," "Dust My Broom," "Give Me One Reason," "Tush," "Pride and Joy," "Stuck in the Middle with You," and "Every Day I Have the Blues."

You have just expanded your repertoire exponentially!

With the ideas in this chapter, you can build bass lines for thousands of songs in any genre and in any key. In the next chapter, you'll learn more ways to vary your arpeggio bass lines.

ARPEGGIO VARIATIONS

The arpeggios you just learned make good bass lines for many blues, rock, and country tunes, but you may find that they get repetitive after a while, especially if you always play them the same way. Following are some ways to take what you've learned and mix it up to make it more interesting.

RHYTHMIC VARIATIONS

You can double the notes in "Kansas City" to make it swing more. Here's an example with the root–3rd–5th–3rd arpeggio.

KANSAS CITY (Doubled)

Words and Music by Jerry Leiber and Mike Stoller

TRACK 26

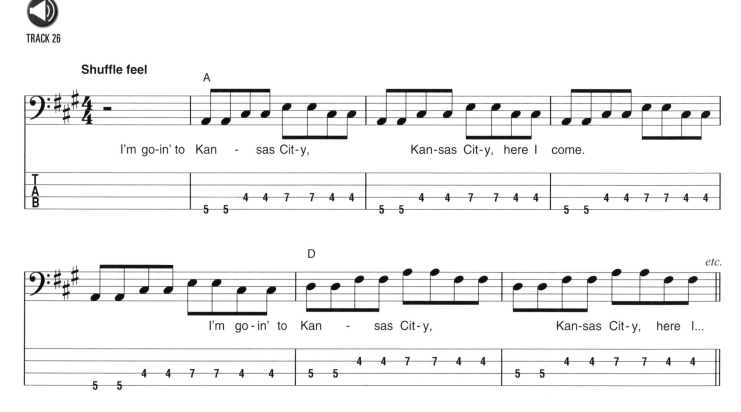

Here's the doubled-up "Kansas City" bass line with the 6th added.

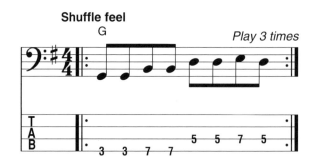

TRACK 26 (cont.)

The next example has some doubled notes and some single notes. It uses the Sea Lion rhythm (1, 2-&, 3, 4-&) from the Rhythm Chart.

TRACK 27

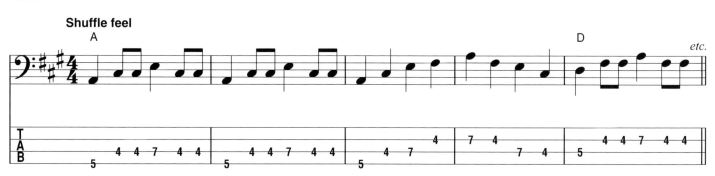

Here's a rhythmic variation of the major arpeggio that was used in hundreds of early rock 'n' roll tunes. You already played a simplified version of it in "Blueberry Hill."

BLUEBERRY HILL (Revisited)

Words and Music by Al Lewis,
Larry Stock and Vincent Rose

TRACK 28

This bass line for "Under the Boardwalk" offers yet another rhythmic variation of the major chord arpeggio. For a change, the pattern is two bars long. Notice the connecting run from G to C in measure 8.

UNDER THE BOARDWALK

Words and Music by Artie Resnick and Kenny Young

TRACK 29

40

This rhythmic variation of the minor arpeggio makes a good bass line for Otis Rush's classic minor-key blues tune "All Your Love (I Miss Loving)."

ALL YOUR LOVE (I MISS LOVING)

Words and Music by Otis Rush

CHANGING THE ORDER OF THE NOTES

You can also vary major and minor arpeggios by playing the notes in a different order. For example, the order of notes in this bass line for "Under the Boardwalk" is root–5th–3rd.

UNDER THE BOARDWALK (Arpeggio Reordering)

Words and Music by Artie Resnick and Kenny Young

TRACK 31

In this version of "All Your Love (I Miss Loving)," the arpeggio notes are reordered to root–5th–♭3rd–5th. In measures 1 and 3, it goes back again to the ♭3rd.

ALL YOUR LOVE (I MISS LOVING)
(Arpeggio Reordering)

Words and Music by Otis Rush

TRACK 32

In the next walking bass line, the tones are ordered root–6th–5th–6th–5th. Notice that beats 1–3 are doubled notes and beat 4 is two different eighth notes.

TRACK 33

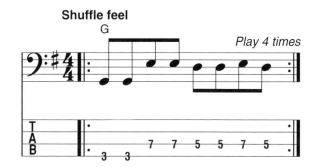

This bass line has a Latin/soul feel, and the arpeggio is ordered root–6th–5th–3rd–5th.

TRACK 33 (cont.)

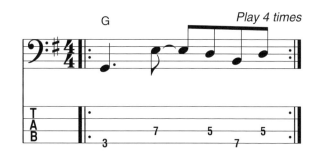

For a change, this one starts on the octave note.

TRACK 33 (cont.)

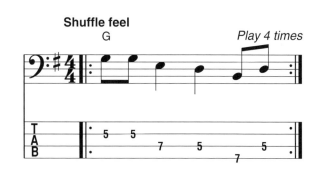

With everything you've learned so far, you can sit in with practically any ukulele meetup or jam session and hold your own, as long as you know what the chords are in any given song. The idea is that you now have tools to use however you like. You can mix them up. Play one part of a song alternating the root and 5th, and play another part using walking bass. You can even take one root note and make it swing just by varying the rhythm. The chapters that follow show you even more ways to become a truly formidable uke bass player.

CHORD PROGRESSIONS: SONGS BY NUMBERS

Chord progression is a fancy term for how chords move in a song. Chords often move in predictable ways, so here you'll take a look at some of the most common patterns.

Why do you need to know about these patterns? Well, if you always read from a book that has the chords written out, you don't. But…

- If you know some of the common patterns in which chords move in songs, you won't freak out every time somebody throws a new song at you—without a book or a chord chart. There's a good chance that "new" song will follow one of the patterns you're about to learn.

- Also, once you know how to play these chord patterns on the fretboard, you'll be able to move them around and play them in any key. Everybody will think you're a musical genius!

DIATONIC HARMONY

Diatonic harmony refers to all the chords that belong to a key. There are seven notes in a major scale, and these notes are numbered 1–2–3–4–5–6–7. A chord can be built on top of each of these notes. Some of these chords are major, some are minor, and one is diminished. Roman numerals are used to refer to the chords in a key, with the major chords being uppercase, the minor chords lowercase, and the diminished chord lowercase followed by a degree symbol (°). For example, in the key of C, the chords are:

I (C) – ii (Dm) – iii (Em) – IV (F) – V (G) – vi (Am) – vii° (B°)

Roman Numeral Review		
I, i	=	1
II, ii	=	2
III, iii	=	3
IV, iv	=	4
V, v	=	5
VI, vi	=	6
VII, vii	=	7

Using this system, you can refer to any chord in a given key. The ii chord ("two chord") in the key of C is Dm, the V chord ("five chord") in the key of C is G, and so on. (Some songs include non-diatonic chords; for example, it's possible for a D major chord [II] to occur in a song that's in the key of C.)

I–IV–V SONGS

While other instruments are playing chords, your job as a bass uke player is to play notes that support those chords; so it's necessary for you to understand how chord progressions work.

Start with one of the most common progressions: I–IV–V. Countless songs in all genres (blues, rock, country, bluegrass, folk, etc.) are three-chord songs with just the I, IV, and V chords. In the key of C, that would be C, F, and G.

You've already learned how to find the 1, 3, 5, and 6 notes of any key, so you know how to get to the roots for the I and V chords. Next, look at how to find the 4th note in a key, which is the root of the IV chord.

HOW TO FIND THE 4TH

There are two easy ways to find the 4th. The first (easiest) way is to go one string higher than the root of the I chord, on the same fret. You don't even have to know which note you're playing; the 4th is always right above the root of the I chord (one string higher/same fret).

Here's an iconic rock chord progression that fits songs like "Louie, Louie," "Twist and Shout," "Wild Thing," "Hang on, Sloopy," most of "Good Lovin'," the verses to "Get Off My Cloud," and many more tunes. In this example, you go from 1 to 4 on open strings. The 5 is fretted at the 2nd fret of the 2nd string, a whole step above the 4. Remember, you are playing the roots of the I, IV, and V chords.

Iconic Rock Progression in A (4th above/same fret)

TRACK 34

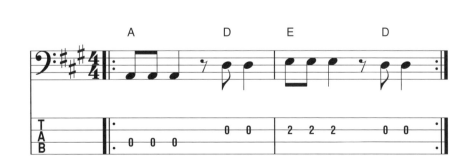

Here's the same progression in the key of C, played on fretted strings with a slightly different rhythm.

Iconic Rock Progression in C (4th above/fretted strings)

TRACK 34 (cont.)

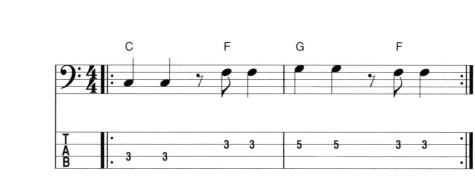

If that's too easy for you, here's another way to find the 4th: It's one string lower and two frets down from the root of the I chord.

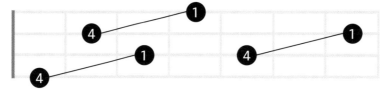

Try the same iconic rock progression using this method of finding the 4th. (Notice you're just varying the rhythms a bit as you go.)

Iconic Rock Progression in C (4th below/two frets down)

TRACK 34 (cont.)

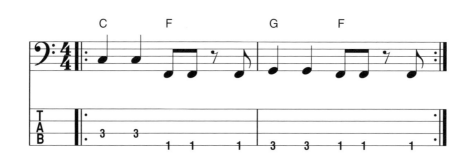

Here's another way to look at it. You already know two ways to find the 5th:

- The 5th is one string lower than the root of the I chord, on the same fret.

- The 5th is one string higher than the root of the I chord, two frets up.

Once you have found the 5th either way, the 4th is always two frets below it.

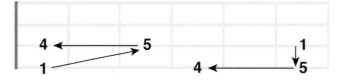

Thousands of classic blues songs also consist of the I, IV, and V chords, and they often occur in a certain order. Songs like "Stormy Monday," "Every Day I Have the Blues," "Pride and Joy," "Kansas City," and "Route 66," plus early rock songs like "Hound Dog," "Whole Lotta Shakin' Goin' On," "Johnny B. Goode," "Blue Suede Shoes," and "Rock around the Clock," all have the I, IV, and V chords in roughly the same order. This order, or pattern of chords, is the **12-bar blues progression**.

TRACK 35

12-BAR BLUES PROGRESSION

In the example above, notice that you're playing an alternating bass pattern using the root and 5th of each chord. Remember, these patterns start with the root of the I chord, the root of the IV chord, and the root of the V chord.

Other well-known three-chord songs include "You Are My Sunshine," "This Land Is Your Land," "Blowin' in the Wind," "Free Fallin'," "Brown Eyed Girl," "King of the Road," "Up Around the Bend," "Me and Bobby McGee," "I Walk the Line," and countless other country, bluegrass, and folk songs.

I–vi–ii–V SONGS

Don't panic! We're just adding a couple of minor chords to the mix, the ii and the vi.

The next most common chord progression after the I–IV–V is the I–vi–ii–V. So many songs follow this pattern that it has been given many nicknames over the years: "ice cream changes," "standard changes," "dime-store progression," and "rhythm changes" (after the Gershwin song "I Got Rhythm").

Here's an easy way to play this progression. It's a movable root pattern that can start with the I chord on any string except the 4th string.

I–vi–ii–V

Here's how it looks with open strings:

I–vi–ii–V (Using Open Strings)

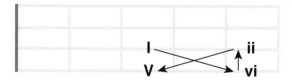

Following is the I–vi–ii–V progression in the keys of A and C with different rhythms.

Rhythm Changes in A

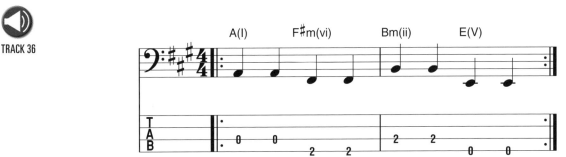

TRACK 36

Rhythm Changes in C

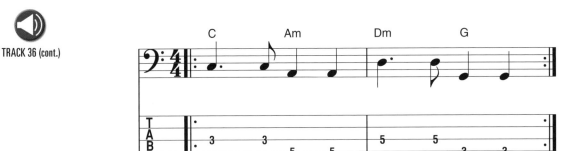

TRACK 36 (cont.)

I–vi–ii–V THROUGH THE DECADES

This progression has been used in songs with many different rhythms and in many different keys. Try playing along with the following tracks.

- 1930s: "Heart and Soul," "Blue Moon," and "I Got Rhythm"

- 1950s: "Teenager in Love," "All I Have to Do Is Dream," and "26 Miles"

- 1960s: "Please, Mr. Postman" and the chorus of "Be My Baby"

- 1980s: "(Everybody's Got a) Hungry Heart" and "Every Breath You Take"

I–V–vi–IV SONGS: ANOTHER ICONIC ROCK PROGRESSION

As the comedic rock group Axis of Awesome point out in their brilliant YouTube video, this is another popular chord progression that underlies many pop songs. You've already played it in "I'm Yours." In most cases, it's not the whole song, but it is the chorus or another big part of the song's structure. Here's how it looks on the bass uke fretboard. It's a movable pattern that can start on the 1st, 2nd, or 3rd string:

I–V–vi–IV

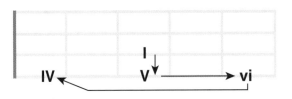

I'M YOURS (Revisited)

Words and Music by Jason Mraz

TRACK 37

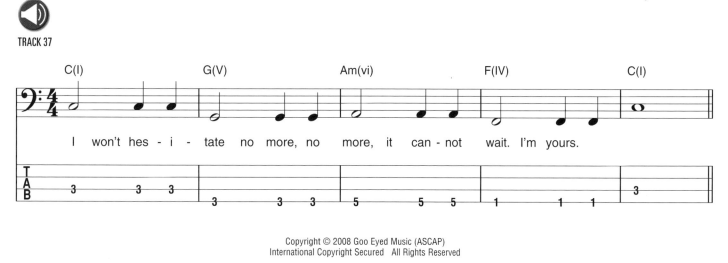

Try this progression on your own in the key of C with "You're Beautiful" (James Blunt), "Happy Ending" (Mika), or "With or Without You" (U2).

If you make the chord changes faster (two chords per bar), they fit songs like "Let It Be" (the Beatles), "Under the Bridge" (Red Hot Chili Peppers), "No Woman, No Cry" (Bob Marley), "Can You Feel the Love Tonight" (Elton John), "Forever Young" (Alphaville), and many more.

I–V–vi–IV (Faster Changes)

TRACK 38

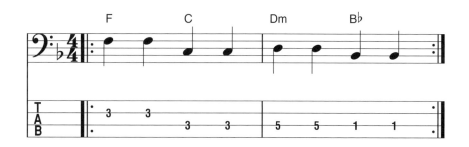

ICONIC BASS LINES

Some popular songs are defined by their instantly recognizable bass lines. Following are some examples. They're fun to play, and you can steal some of them to use in other songs that have a similar rhythmic feel.

Carol Kaye is one of the famous "Wrecking Crew" musicians who backed up numerous pop bands in the 1960s and '70s. Her bass line for Sonny and Cher's hit "The Beat Goes On" is the signature lick of that tune.

THE BEAT GOES ON

Words and Music by Sonny Bono

TRACK 39

Here's the bass line to the famous soul hit "Stand by Me" by Ben E. King.

STAND BY ME

Words and Music by Jerry Leiber,
Mike Stoller and Ben E. King

TRACK 40

The Four Tops' 1965 soul song "I Can't Help Myself" also has a defining bass line. In 1966, Los Bravos used the same bass line in their hit "Black Is Black." See what we mean about "stealing" popular bass lines?

I CAN'T HELP MYSELF (SUGAR PIE, HONEY BUNCH)

Words and Music by Brian Holland,
Lamont Dozier and Edward Holland Jr.

TRACK 41

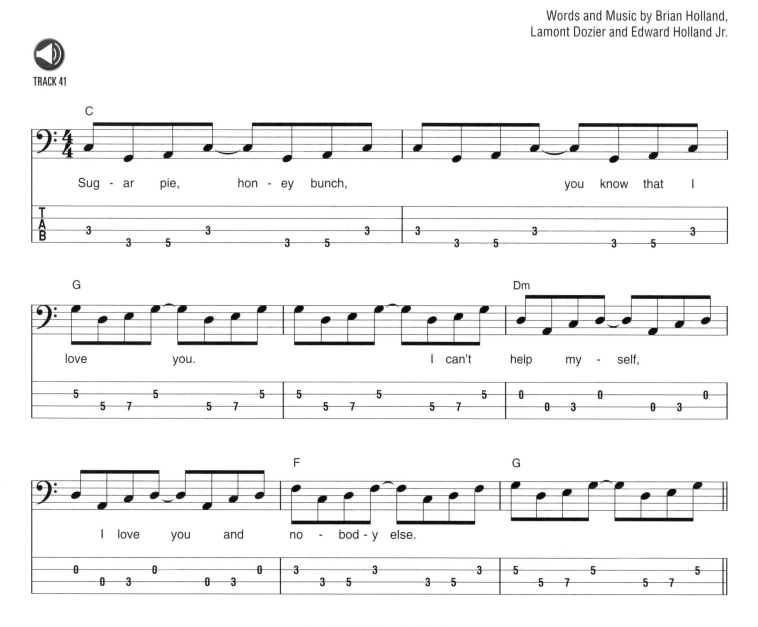

Albert King's "Born Under a Bad Sign" has this distinctive bass line:

BORN UNDER A BAD SIGN

Words and Music by Booker T. Jones and William Bell

TRACK 42

Rick James's 1981 "Super Freak" had such a cool, funky bass line that MC Hammer used it nine years later in his hit "U Can't Touch This."

SUPER FREAK

Words and Music by Rick James and Alonzo Miller

TRACK 43

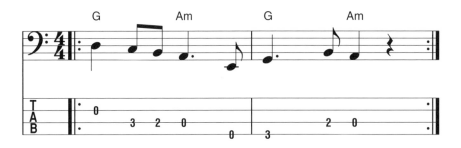

There are many more popular songs with defining bass lines. Listen to Pink Floyd's "Money," the White Stripes' "Seven Nation Army," Cream's "Sunshine of Your Love," the Beatles' "Come Together," the Red Hot Chili Peppers' "Give It Away," Queen's "Another One Bites the Dust," Michael Jackson's "Billie Jean," and James Brown's "I Got You (I Feel Good)." Also, just for a change, listen to a bass line played by a bass ukulele in the Ukulele Orchestra of Great Britain's version of "Higher and Higher."

RHYTHM GROOVES

The material in this chapter is for the more adventurous bass uke players; it may be more advanced than what's been covered so far, but whether or not you understand the theory behind these different grooves, you may find them fun to play.

Whatever the genre (blues, rock, country, etc.), songs have different rhythmic feels or grooves. As a bass player, you'll be better equipped to play with other people if you know some bass parts that go with the following common grooves.

CUT TIME: BLUEGRASS, COUNTRY, AND POP

This groove uses cut time and has a "boom-chick-a" feel. Remember, in cut time, the note values are cut in half; so, a whole note lasts for two beats, a half note lasts for one beat, a quarter note lasts for a half of a beat, and so on. This cut-time feel can be heard in many classic country and bluegrass tunes, including some you've already played, like "Jambalaya." In that tune, you played alternating bass on the root and 5th. "Wagon Wheel" has the same groove, but you will play only the root notes.

WAGON WHEEL

Words and Music by Bob Dylan and Ketch Secor

TRACK 44

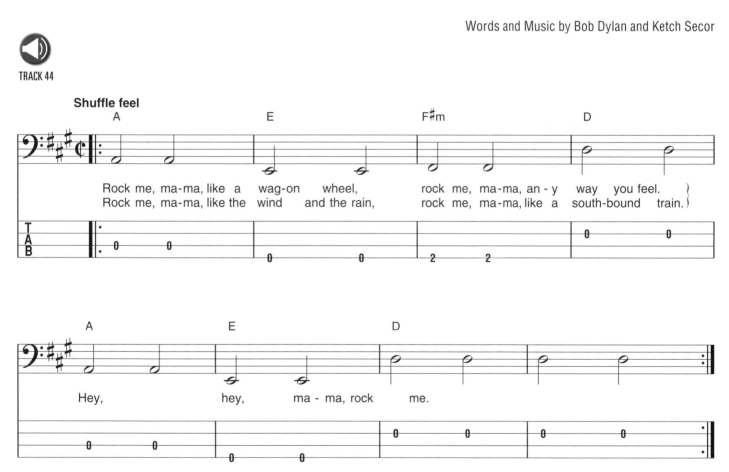

There are cut-time pop tunes as well, like Bruno Mars' "Count on Me." This arrangement includes alternating bass on the C and Em chords.

COUNT ON ME

Words and Music by Bruno Mars,
Ari Levine and Philip Lawrence

TRACK 45

ROCK BALLAD

Here's a bass pattern for "Hey Jude" by the Beatles. You can play a similar pattern for other rock ballads like "Helpless," "You're Beautiful," "Wild Horses," "I Shall Be Released," and "Hello."

HEY JUDE

TRACK 46

Words and Music by John Lennon and Paul McCartney

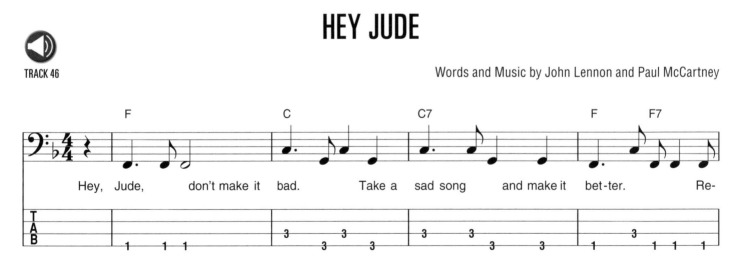

mem-ber   to   let her un-der your skin,   then you be-gin   to make it   bet - ter.

SHUFFLE BEAT

A feel-good rhythm groove in rock, blues, and country tunes, the shuffle beat has that bump-ba-bump-ba-bump feel we discussed earlier in the book. You can hear this groove in songs like "Bad, Bad Leroy Brown," "Heartache Tonight," "Your Mama Don't Dance," and "La Grange." You've already played a shuffle beat in "Kansas City" with bass patterns like the one below.

TRACK 47

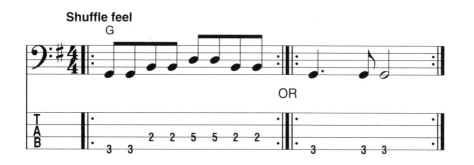

STRAIGHT-EIGHTHS ROCK BEAT

This is the most common rock beat. It's called "straight eighths" because the drummer usually plays eighth notes, evenly, on the cymbal or hi-hat (ding-ding-ding-ding-ding-ding-ding-ding). The bass can play all eighth notes. Listen to the difference between this straight-eighths pattern and the "Kansas City" bass pattern above. The notation is identical, but the feel is different. This groove works for "Proud Mary," "Johnny B. Goode," and a thousand other rock tunes.

TRACK 48

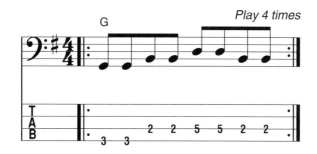

Adele's "Rolling in the Deep" is a classic example of the straight-eighths feel. The bass plays eight eighth notes per bar.

ROLLING IN THE DEEP

Words and Music by Adele Adkins and Paul Epworth

TRACK 49

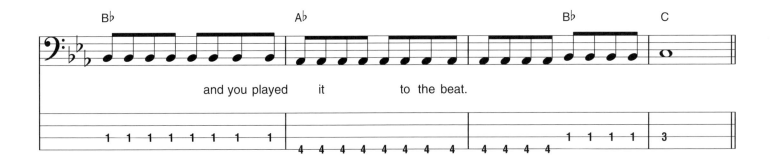

There are endless ways to vary the straight-eighths beat. If you leave some space in your bass pattern, you can get a relaxed rock feel as in "Margaritaville"; you can also get a Latin feel as in "Blue Bayou" or some of the tunes you've already played, like "Under the Boardwalk" and "Stand by Me."

TRACK 50

WALTZ TIME

A waltz has three beats in each measure instead of four, as in "Sweet Baby James" (James Taylor), "Norwegian Wood" (The Beatles), "The Tennessee Waltz," "Breakaway" (Kelly Clarkson), and "Piano Man" (Billy Joel). Often in waltzes, the bass simply plays root notes on the first beat of each measure, like the following example.

TRACK 51

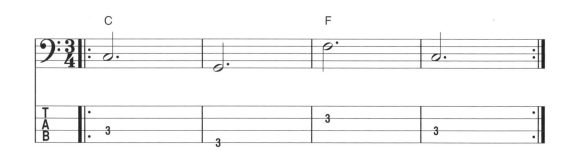

6/8 TIME

In 6/8 time, there are six beats in each measure, as in "House of the Rising Sun," "I Can't Help Falling in Love," and Ed Sheeran's "Perfect." In this rhythmic feel, the bass often plays root notes on the first and sixth beats, or on the first, fifth, and sixth beats.

PERFECT

Words and Music by Ed Sheeran

TRACK 52

STRAIGHT-FOUR TIME

This rhythm groove has four beats to the bar, as in "Hi-Heel Sneakers," "Bread and Butter," "Big Boss Man," and "The Boy from New York City."

TRACK 53

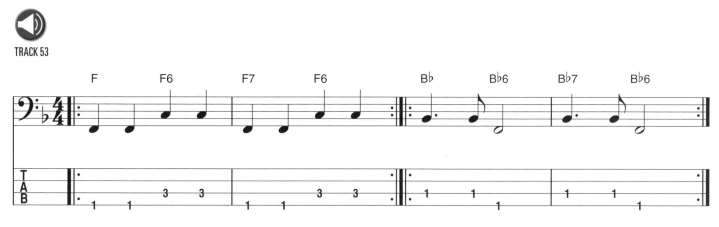

FUNK

Funk beats originated in soul music and rhythm 'n' blues, but rockers use them as well. In funk music, the bass tends to break up the rhythm into sixteenth notes, which leads to sophisticated, syncopated patterns. **Syncopation** is a rhythmic device in which emphasis is given to offbeats or the normally "weaker" parts of a beat. A perfect example of this is in measure 4 of the example below. There is an eighth note on the "&" of beat 2, followed by a rest on the downbeat of beat 3, and two sixteenth notes on "& a." An arranger of this type of music once said that R&B and funk bass players think like conga drummers. Classic funk tunes include "Superstition," "Give Up the Funk," "I'll Take You There," "Brick House," and "Rock Steady." Try some of these cool funk patterns.

TRACK 54

After you've played the tunes or exercises in this chapter, listen to some of your favorite songs and see whether each one matches up with one of the grooves covered here. Maybe you can make up bass parts that fit the songs you like by imitating the patterns you've just studied.

THE "P WORD" (PRACTICE)

Let's face it. Practicing can be boring—it's not sexy, not exciting, but it is *the* thing that will make you great. You can get anywhere you want to go on bass with just one task—practice—especially if you do it right.

To get really good at this, start small and start simple.

According to neurologists, here's the most efficient way to practice:

Short, Frequent Intervals

Research has shown that shorter, more frequent intervals work better than sitting down for hours at a time. Fifteen minutes a few times a day works better than one long block of time.

Forget What You Just Practiced!

This sounds nuts, but research bears out that the best way to learn something is to practice it only a few times and then move on to the next thing. Each time you come back and recall a skill, after forgetting it, it gets imbedded in your brain more firmly!

Set Goals

Each time you sit down to practice, have a goal. There are three types of goals:

- **Small goals:** These are very specific, such as focusing on the placement of your finger on the fretboard to get a clear tone from a single note.

- **Larger goals:** For example, work on making one difficult measure smooth.

- **Still larger goals:** Pick a bass part you want to focus on and try to play it smoothly.

A Suggested Practice Plan

1. Practice a little every day.

2. Warm up by reviewing some bass lines that you already know and are easy for you.

3. Practice one or two new bass lines or skills that are new material.

Play with People, or Play Along with Recordings

Practice with someone who plays a "chording" instrument, like ukulele, guitar, piano, or accordion. If no playing partner is handy, play along with recordings. It helps you keep time—and don't stop when you make a mistake, just keep going. There are free practice tracks on YouTube, in all genres, and they usually spell out the chord progressions; plus, you can slow these videos down to make them easier to play along with.

A FINAL NOTE

It really is "all about that *bass*."

Once again, you are the foundation. Everything else is built on what you do. While others in the group may be shredding and doing all sorts of fancy strums and picking, you not only *get by* with simple bass lines, but you are also appreciated for it. Bass lines that are too busy can drive the other players nuts. As long as you keep that groove steady and strong, you are golden!

This is not to say that you can't get fancy too. There's always... the bass solo! And trust me, if you take a solo, you will get more applause than anyone else!

ABOUT THE AUTHORS

Lynn Sokolow has been playing stand-up bass with the ukulele community ever since her husband Fred Sokolow carried her over the uke threshold! Although she began in her twenties, playing electric bass in rock and R&B bands (and currently plays upright bass in several bluegrass bands), Lynn has since come to her senses and jumped onboard with bass ukulele. She has taught bass ukulele at uke festivals all over the world. Her primary focus in all of her musical endeavors is to generate as much fun out of playing as is humanly possible, and this is her philosophy when it comes to teaching.

Fred Sokolow is best known as the author of over 200 instructional and transcription books and DVDs for guitar, banjo, Dobro, lap steel, mandolin, and ukulele. Fred has long been a well-known West Coast multi-string performer and recording artist, particularly on the acoustic music scene. The diverse musical genres covered in his books and DVDs—along with the bluegrass, jazz, and rock CDs he has released—demonstrate his mastery of many musical styles. Whether he's playing Hawaiian hulas, Delta bottleneck blues, bluegrass or old-time banjo, '30s swing guitar, or screaming rock solos, he does it with authenticity and passion.

Fred also wrote or co-wrote:

Fretboard Roadmaps for Bass, book/soundfiles, Hal Leonard

Fretboard Roadmaps for Ukulele, book/soundfiles, Hal Leonard

Fretboard Roadmaps for Baritone Ukulele, book/soundfiles, Hal Leonard

101 Tips for Ukulele, Hal Leonard

Slide & Slack Key Ukulele, book/soundfiles, Hal Leonard

Fingerstyle Ukulele, book/soundfiles, Hal Leonard

Jazzing Up the Ukulele, book/CD, Flea Market Music Inc., distributed by Hal Leonard

Ragtime Fingerstyle Ukulele, book/soundfiles, Hal Leonard

Bluegrass Ukulele, book/CD, Flea Market Music Inc., distributed by Hal Leonard

Blues Ukulele, book/CD, Flea Market Music Inc., distributed by Hal Leonard

The Beatles for Fingerstyle Ukulele, book, Hal Leonard

Christmas Songs for Solo Fingerstyle Ukulele, book, Hal Leonard

Disney Songs for Fingerstyle Ukulele, book, Hal Leonard

Email Fred with any questions about these or his other uke, guitar, banjo, and mandolin books at: Sokolowmusic.com.

HAL·LEONARD® UKULELE PLAY-ALONG

1. POP HITS
00701451 Book/CD Pack $15.99

3. HAWAIIAN FAVORITES
00701453 Book/Online Audio $14.99

4. CHILDREN'S SONGS
00701454 Book/Online Audio $14.99

5. CHRISTMAS SONGS
00701696 Book/CD Pack $12.99

6. LENNON & MCCARTNEY
00701723 Book/Online Audio $12.99

7. DISNEY FAVORITES
00701724 Book/Online Audio $14.99

8. CHART HITS
00701745 Book/CD Pack $15.99

9. THE SOUND OF MUSIC
00701784 Book/CD Pack $14.99

10. MOTOWN
00701964 Book/CD Pack $12.99

11. CHRISTMAS STRUMMING
00702458 Book/Online Audio $12.99

12. BLUEGRASS FAVORITES
00702584 Book/CD Pack $12.99

13. UKULELE SONGS
00702599 Book/CD Pack $12.99

14. JOHNNY CASH
00702615 Book/Online Audio $15.99

15. COUNTRY CLASSICS
00702834 Book/CD Pack $12.99

16. STANDARDS
00702835 Book/CD Pack $12.99

17. POP STANDARDS
00702836 Book/CD Pack $12.99

18. IRISH SONGS
00703086 Book/Online Audio $12.99

19. BLUES STANDARDS
00703087 Book/CD Pack $12.99

20. FOLK POP ROCK
00703088 Book/CD Pack $12.99

21. HAWAIIAN CLASSICS
00703097 Book/CD Pack $12.99

22. ISLAND SONGS
00703098 Book/CD Pack $12.99

23. TAYLOR SWIFT
00221966 Book/Online Audio $16.99

24. WINTER WONDERLAND
00101871 Book/CD Pack $12.99

25. GREEN DAY
00110398 Book/CD Pack $14.99

26. BOB MARLEY
00110399 Book/Online Audio $14.99

27. TIN PAN ALLEY
00116358 Book/CD Pack $12.99

28. STEVIE WONDER
00116736 Book/CD Pack $14.99

29. OVER THE RAINBOW & OTHER FAVORITES
00117076 Book/Online Audio $15.99

30. ACOUSTIC SONGS
00122336 Book/CD Pack $14.99

31. JASON MRAZ
00124166 Book/CD Pack $14.99

32. TOP DOWNLOADS
00127507 Book/CD Pack $14.99

33. CLASSICAL THEMES
00127892 Book/Online Audio $14.99

34. CHRISTMAS HITS
00128602 Book/CD Pack $14.99

35. SONGS FOR BEGINNERS
00129009 Book/Online Audio $14.99

36. ELVIS PRESLEY HAWAII
00138199 Book/Online Audio $14.99

37. LATIN
00141191 Book/Online Audio $14.99

38. JAZZ
00141192 Book/Online Audio $14.99

39. GYPSY JAZZ
00146559 Book/Online Audio $15.99

40. TODAY'S HITS
00160845 Book/Online Audio $14.99

HAL·LEONARD®

www.halleonard.com

Learn to play the
Ukulele
with these great Hal Leonard books!

Hal Leonard Ukulele Method

Book 1
by Lil' Rev

The Hal Leonard Ukulele Method is designed for anyone just learning to play ukulele. This comprehensive and easy-to-use beginner's guide by acclaimed performer and uke master Lil' Rev includes many fun songs of different styles to learn and play. The accompanying audio contains 46 tracks of songs for demonstration and play along. Includes: types of ukuleles, tuning, music reading, melody playing, chords, strumming, scales, tremolo, music notation and tablature, a variety of music styles, ukulele history and much more.

00695847	Book Only	$8.99
00695832	Book/Online Audio	$12.99
00320534	DVD	$14.99

Book 2

00695948	Book Only	$7.99
00695949	Book/Online Audio	$11.99

Ukulele Chord Finder

00695803	9" x 12"	$8.99
00695902	6" x 9"	$7.99
00696472	Book 1 with Online Audio + Chord Finder	$16.99

Ukulele Scale Finder

00696378	9" x 12"	$8.99

Easy Songs for Ukulele

00695904	Book/Online Audio	$16.99
00695905	Book	$9.99

Ukulele for Kids

00696468	Book/Online Audio	$14.99
00244855	Method & Songbook	$22.99

Baritone Ukulele Method – Book 1

00696564	Book/Online Audio	$12.99

Jake Shimabukuro Teaches Ukulele Lessons

Learn notes, chords, songs, and playing techniques from the master of modern ukulele! In this unique book with online video, Jake Shimabukuro will get you started on playing the ukulele. The book includes full transcriptions of every example, the video features Jake teaching you everything you need to know plus video of Jake playing all the examples.
00320992 Book/Online Video $22.99

Fretboard Roadmaps – Ukulele

The Essential Patterns That All the Pros Know and Use
by Fred Sokolow & Jim Beloff

Take your uke playing to the next level! Tunes and exercises in standard notation and tab illustrate each technique. Absolute beginners can follow the diagrams and instruction step-by-step, while intermediate and advanced players can use the chapters non-sequentially to increase their understanding of the ukulele. The audio includes 59 demo and play-along tracks.
00695901 Book/Online Audio $15.99

Play Ukulele Today!

A Complete Guide to the Basics
by Barrett Tagliarino

This is the ultimate self-teaching method for ukulele! Includes audio with full demo tracks and over 60 great songs. You'll learn: care for the instrument; how to produce sound; reading music notation and rhythms; and more.

00699638	Book/Online Audio	$12.99
00293927	Book 1 & 2/Online Media	$19.99

Ukulele Aerobics

For All Levels, from Beginner to Advanced
by Chad Johnson

This package provides practice material for every day of the week and includes an online audio access code for all the workouts in the book. Techniques covered include: strumming, fingerstyle, slides, bending, damping, vibrato, tremolo and more.
00102162 Book/Online Audio $19.99

All About Ukulele

A Fun and Simple Guide to Playing Ukulele
by Chad Johnson

If you wish there was a fun and engaging way to motivate you in your uke playing quest, then this is it: All About Ukulele is for you. Whether it's learning to read music, playing in a band, finding the right instrument, or all of the above, this enjoyable guide will help you.

00233655 Book/Online Audio $19.99

HAL•LEONARD®
www.halleonard.com

Prices, contents and availability subject to change without notice. Prices listed in U.S. funds.